The Unspoken Effects of Hair Loss

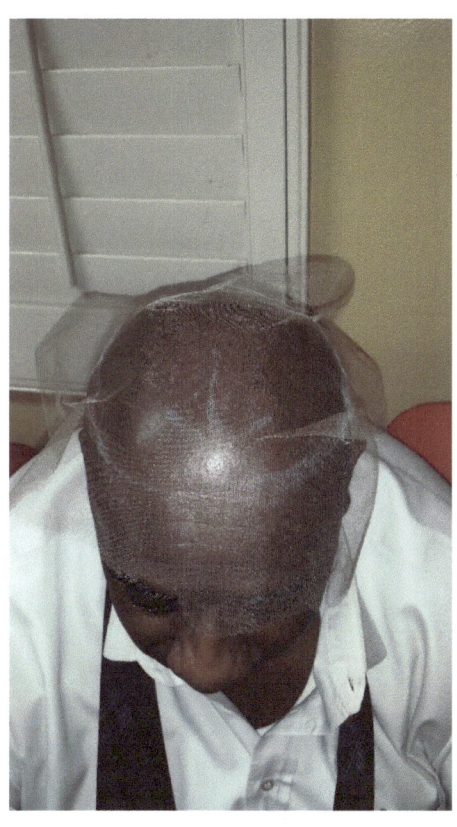

Dedication

This book is dedicated to my beautiful cousin

Candice Marie Howard. Your memory still lives

within us as we try to be the best we can be and

make the most of the time we have. We will forever

love you!

Acknowledgement

I would like to acknowledge the friends and family

that believed in me, and encouraged me to bring

forth this book. I would like to personally thank Mr.

Gil for being there every step of the way.

Table of Contents

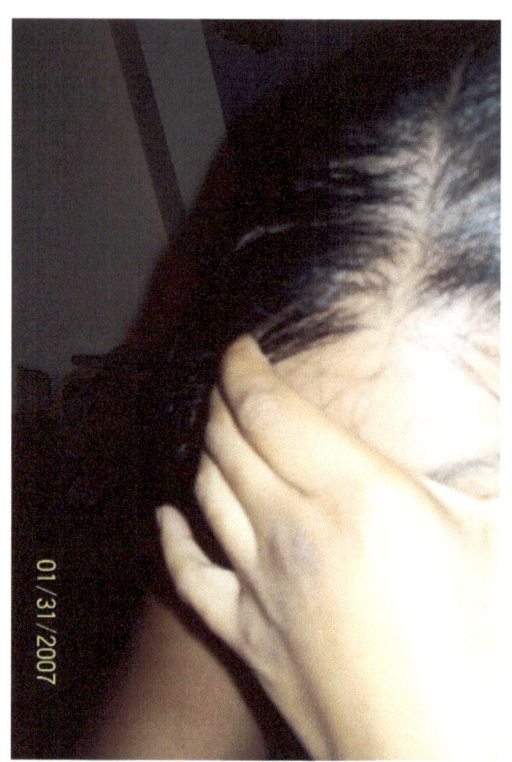

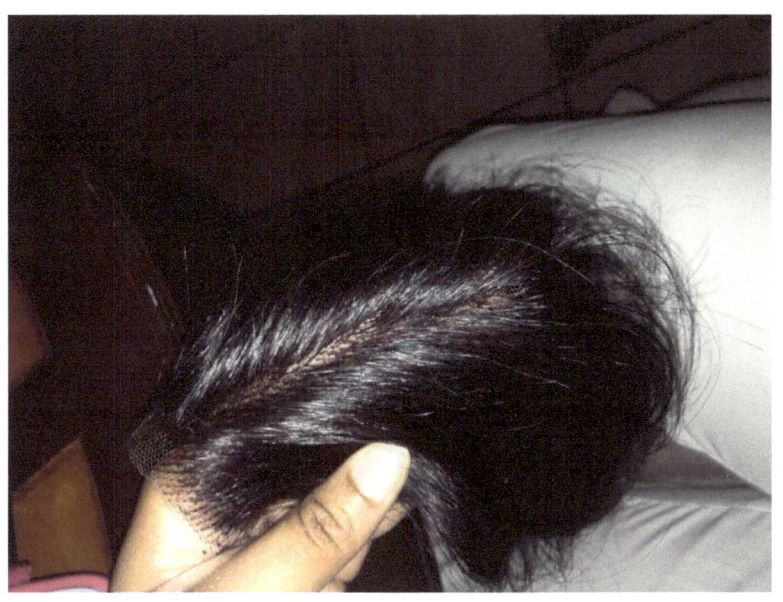

Introduction

We've all been exposed to it at some point.

Hair loss. Although we understand what it is, we don't know every effect it can have on an individual. Because people's makeup is different from one another, hair loss can affect people in different ways. In this book, you will be introduced to some of the things that are not talked about or discussed when it comes to hair loss, and you may even be able to help someone who is experiencing some of these things, cope with it, or get through the tougher times.

What Is Hair Loss?

We've all seen the physical effects of hair loss.

We've seen a few thinning hairlines, balding rooftops, so we pretty much think of hair loss in the aspect of balding in older people.

But, hair loss can be due to many factors.

Hair loss can be due to health, and different medical treatments such as Chemotherapy, radiation, and even some medications.

Hair loss can even be due to too much tension on the hair follicles, and can even be hereditary. Hair loss can be described as the loss of your natural growing hair.

Who Is Affected By Hair Loss?

According to the American Hair loss Council, they estimate that the total male population affected by hair loss is:

- Ages 18-29: 7.3 million/ 30 percent

- Ages 29-39: 8.2 million/ 40 percent

- Ages 40-49: 6.9 million/ 45 percent

- Ages 50-59: 5.7 million/ 55 percent

- Ages 60-69: 5.5 million/ 65 percent

It is estimated that a total of 33.6 million males are affected by hair loss.

The total female population estimated with hair loss is:

- Ages 20-29: 2.4 million/ 12 percent

- Ages 30-39: 6 million / 29 percent

- Ages 40-49: 5.7 million / 36 percent

- Ages 50-59: 3 million/ 27 percent

- Ages 60-69: 2.4 million/ 21 percent

It is estimated that there are 19.5 million females who are affected by hair loss.

These estimates didn't take into consideration children affected by hair loss under the age of 18. Children can experience hair loss due to a hereditary condition,

Chemotherapy, radiation, burns, pulling out of

one's hair, etc.

Really, anyone can be affected by hair loss at some

point.

The Emotional Side of Hair Loss

Hair loss can have a tremendous impact on a person's emotional health and well-being. Just think about it, when you approach someone

Who is experiencing hair loss, a lot of times they are not willingly displaying it. Certain men will try to hide thinning areas by combing existing hair over the thin areas, which is where we get the term "the comb-over". This is an emotional gesture, because they don't want anyone to know that

They are experiencing hair loss.

A lot of people who are experiencing hair loss will never tell. And if you're fortunate enough to know someone who will talk about their

Feelings with hair loss, you can help them through it. They may experience low self-esteem levels, and their self-confidence levels may even be lowered due to the hair loss, and the idea that they are being stared at.

Some individuals may even be in a state of denial because they don't want to accept their hair loss condition.

They don't want to accept it because there have been many jokes about hair loss, and many people view it as a negative and unnatural occurrence that they would not want to be a part of. So it is easier

just to deny and hide the condition.

Another emotion they may experience is fear. They

are afraid that someone will point it out publicly.

They may even shy away from the hair replacement

experience in fear that their hair piece will be

unnatural and "noticeably fake".

Some people may even feel like since the onset of

their hair loss, that they may not be as healthy as

they once were. That tie into the ideas people have

wrapped around hair loss.

Let the Uplifting Begin

With today's technology, there are many options for hair replacement.

There are surgical and non-surgical options to hair replacement.

Today, you can almost walk into any salon and find a non-surgical alternative for hair replacement. The options that we see now, have a level of realness that has the ability to mimic a person's own natural hair patterns.

Take for instance, the non-surgical alternative of a Lace wig. If constructed of high quality materials, with the hair placement strategically placed with the utmost attention to detail, it can appear as if there is no hair alteration being worn.

Hairpiece manufacturers understand the importance of a natural looking piece, so they take this into consideration each time they enter the creation stage.

Now that we know a little bit about some of the effects of hair loss, and some solutions, we want to be mindful of how we deal with hair loss.

We don't want anyone to feel like we are taking pity on them, or we view them in a different way than we used to. If we know someone who is struggling with their self-esteem after the onset of hair loss, we want to be able to help them understand that it is a natural thing, and that they aren't thought of any different than they were before. It is important to help build someone's self-esteem level, and something as small as a "you did a good job today" can work wonders.

If you notice your loved one or friend making an effort to conceal their thinning areas and still look nice, compliment them.

For example, "that is a nice scarf", or "what a cool hat you have on".

These are just a few little things we can do to help uplift someone.

About the Author

My name is Markeasha Moore. I am a licensed cosmetologist who is passionate about making a person look as good as they want to feel. I have a strong desire in working with individuals suffering from hair loss, because I understand the emotional toll it can have on a person's life. I have 12 years' experience with hairpiece making, 7 years' experience in ventilating, and 7 years focusing on non-surgical hair replacement. I only use high quality materials to ensure that detection is very minimal to none at all. I keep in mind the breathability of the hairpiece for maximum health and comfort. I cater to all nationalities, and my services are tailored specifically to each individual. If you are interested in seeing what I have to offer in hair replacement, visit me at realistically-yours.com.

Disclaimer

This book is not designed to treat or diagnose any condition. The views in this book are specifically of the author's and the author's opinions.

--Markeasha Moore